Tongue Lyre

CRAB ORCHARD SERIES IN POETRY
FIRST BOOK AWARD

Tongue
Lyre

Tyler Mills

CRAB ORCHARD REVIEW &

SOUTHERN ILLINOIS

UNIVERSITY PRESS

CARBONDALE

AND EDWARDSVILLE

16 15 14 13   4 3 2 1

The Crab Orchard Series in Poetry is a joint publishing
venture of Southern Illinois University Press and *Crab
Orchard Review*. This series has been made possible by the
generous support of the Office of the President of Southern
Illinois University and the Office of the Vice Chancellor
for Academic Affairs and Provost at Southern Illinois
University Carbondale.

Crab Orchard Series in Poetry Editor: Jon Tribble
First Book Award Judge for 2011: Lee Ann Roripaugh

Library of Congress Cataloging-in-Publication Data
Mills, Tyler, 1983–
  [Poems. Selections]
  Tongue lyre : poems / by Tyler Mills.
      pages   cm. — (Crab Orchard Series in Poetry)
  Crab Orchard Series in Poetry First Book Award.
  ISBN 978-0-8093-3222-9 (paperback : alk. paper)
  ISBN 0-8093-3222-1 (paperback : alk. paper)
  ISBN 978-0-8093-3223-6 (ebook) (print)
  ISBN 0-8093-3223-X (ebook) (print)
  I. Title.
  PS3613.I56994T66 2013
  811Ð.6—dc23   2012038581

Printed on recycled paper. ♻

The paper used in this publication meets the minimum
requirements of American National Standard for
Information Sciences—Permanence of Paper for
Printed Library Materials, ANSI Z39.48-1992. ∞

Contents

Acknowledgments

Many thanks to the editors of the following journals where these poems first appeared, sometimes as slightly different versions:

2River View ("Aiolos and the Bag of Winds" and "Telemachos")
32 Poems ("Standing Still")
Antioch Review ("After the Lotus" and "Water Ballad")
Best New Poets 2007 ("Violin Shop")
Cimarron Review ("Proteus" and "Tell Me, Muse")
Connotation Press ("Oracle")
Crab Orchard Review ("Ossuary" and "Tinsel Halo," chosen for the 2009 Richard Peterson Poetry Prize)
Georgia Review ("In the Chapter 'Rodin in Love'")
Great River Review ("Violinist")
Indiana Review ("Edith Wharton's *Age of Innocence* by T. C. Mills" and "Violin Shop")
Memorious: A Journal of New Verse and Fiction ("Cyclops" and "Nestor")
Nashville Review ("The Sirens")
Spoon River Poetry Review ("Kalypso")
Third Coast ("Performance," chosen for the 2008 *Third Coast* Poetry Prize)
TriQuarterly Online ("Penelope's Firebird Weft")
Water~Stone Review ("Odyssey")

When noted, poems draw from these works:

Joyce, James. *Ulysses*. New York: Vintage Books, 1986.
Lattimore, Richmond, trans. *The Odyssey of Homer*. New York: Perennial Classics, 1999.
Ovid. *Metamorphoses*. Trans. Charles Martin. New York: W. W. Norton & Company, 2005.

~

It is with deep gratitude that I thank my teachers for their generosity and for believing in these poems: Elizabeth Arnold, Michael Collier, Cynthia Hogue, Richard Jackson, Shara McCallum, Stanley Plumly, Christina Pugh, and Michael Waters.

I would especially like to thank Stanley Plumly for mentoring this project through its many phases.

I am deeply grateful to Lee Ann Roripaugh for selecting my manuscript for the Crab Orchard Series in Poetry First Book Award. I would also like to thank Jon Tribble, Allison Joseph, and the *Crab Orchard Review* staff for their invaluable editorial work. Many thanks also go to Karl Kageff, Hannah K. New, and everyone at Southern Illinois University Press for making this book possible.

It is with deep gratitude that I thank my parents for their love and support, and my brother and sister for their friendship. I thank my friends for everything they have taught me. And last, I thank Arik deeply, for his love.

~

My reader, this book is for you.

Imprisoned here, my voice will fill the trees
                    —*Philomela*

Tongue

The problem is not night—people gathering in booths—or a game
where you select who to save from an apartment that's on fire.

But at night, the silver bathroom stalls in the Multiplex crack open
as if I am the last horse to wander out during the credits.

What I mean is, my thighs sometimes still feel like the whites
    of a poached egg.
There is logic to thinking about digger wasps, solitary insects
    that excavate

nests from the soil and then straddle their prey, usually an August cricket,
ashy as the blade of a waterlogged feather. And at night, the hermit thrush

calls, flutters to a new tree, calls, and soon the grove hosts a quorum
of these nightingale songs when there is only one traveling from tree
    to tree,

to an oak like the one shading my porch—I go there at night to breathe.
In the myth of Philomela, the King puts his knife down Philomela's throat

after he finishes, then cuts her tongue out. Before she becomes a thrush,
she weaves what happened: images in a bolt of cloth, a kind of flag.

The newspaper pays for them, the flickering paper flags
leaning on the bottom panel of the doors in the neighborhoods.

Again this year, before dawn, the truck door slammed—I heard
someone cross the street. When I woke, flames were mouthing the air.

Edith Wharton's *Age of Innocence* by T. C. Mills

New Year's Eve in Central Park: the flat lake an apricot
before Lucky Cheng's where our transvestite waitress

brings a crown of balloons pinched and twisted
like circus dogs. How quiet we get when they dance,

these new women laying their hands down their flat thighs
and rose feathers trailing from silver heels. *Real, real*:

the age of innocence begins in an opera box
and ends with a dark-haired woman's apartment

window. Or the age of innocence begins with my cousin
holding a green razor between her legs

in my bedroom after not eating the Easter cake
we made with egg whites and almonds,

my hair wrapped in a fist at my neck.
Or the age of innocence begins with rehearsing

Wagner, violins lost in *Tristan und Isolde*, the conductor's hands
pulling the shirt off no one in front of him.

Tell Me, Muse

The child's room balances single beds, mine, my friend's.
Ship curtains enclose the window in blue light.
I bring my violin to the chapped sand slopes
along the Boardwalk fence: thin stripe of beach,

same tide in the morning as evening when the jumper plane pulls
sky with a ribbon of advertisements, omens we stop
talking to read. Along the beach, men replace planks of wood
that had rot through winter, and I notice the homes

nailed shut with plywood as though the ocean will soon
swell like a body breathing in. I stretch out on my blanket.
                                                            Breathe.
My teacher would clap her hands under the instrument's scroll.
There is a story. You are traveling from one place to the return,

do you hear this? Back again. Listen. As though you never left,
as though you can return.
                        My friend joins me with her backpack,
drizzling forest green yarn between her calves. She knits rows of loops,
pulls them out, then goes inside to shower.

So many people in that house. I barely know the couple
that drinks Diet Coke by the liter and argues.
These shore towns are palisades of concrete—
one house dropping its shadow over a smaller one

where the front lawn would be. The chain-link fences
wrapping around each plot glisten in the pink evenings, seeming
to move with restless silver cats. Somewhere someone burns meat.
Go to the gift shop, find your name on a key chain, set it swinging,

and touch the rim of a purple hat—it will behave like a good idea,
propped up on a metal stand. A child will whine outside
the open doorway: *I want, I want.* In my dream,
the ocean swirls to the house. I climb out the window.

Our beds float, rafts too far to reach. I'm on the roof,
the shingles shrinking at my feet. I am going to drown here
with my violin inside, somewhere below me in the bedroom.
We are going to drown—
                              I try to wake my friend,

make tea, sit by the window on a pearly chair. Rain.
I am at the part in my book when Stinking Lizaveta,
shoved against the shed, or held down in the mud—but no one sees,
woman, O woman. Outside the kitchen, the ocean rolls and rolls.

Odyssey

Stained wood homes line the Susquehanna River
like rusted and abandoned train cars. Except—
look: windows glow gold squares in the rain,
baskets of rooms cradling the shadows
moving inside like wings warming smooth dark eggs.
A Winnebago pulls a rickety carousel,
the kind churches rent for town festivals.
Metal green & orange & lilac hooves
jostle above the road, past the granite outcrop,
the quilts for sale hanging above front porches
like sheets blotted brown with tight roses of blood.

Mennonite women wearing oyster-shell bonnets
wait with their husbands for the doctor.
Under the TV, they sit straight-backed,
watching me brush through the doors—*another one.*
Downstairs, faded curtains groom the test room
into separate spaces like a community
theatre. My nurse inspects the form
longer than she needs to, her latex gloves
pausing with the needle, an accusing pen
marking my arms that just lay there, again . . .

Something is about to disappear.
On Route 15, the rusted Winnebago pulls
its tangled bracelet of horses. Painted,
wild eyes watch through the reined net, stiff tassels,
the bare shoulders scalloped with undergarment straps.
I drive past the jumbled shapes of animals
tethered to poles. There is nothing to unhook—
when one horse collapses as though from a hanger,
lying in the road like a long brown deer,
men in tangerine hats pull legs to the curb,
hug the slender neck, saw the head off, and keep it.

Telemachos

There is a sound—a fist? I see the man
in my mind wearing a sweatshirt,
his hood pulled over a red hat.
Orange sun moves over cars,
warms the under-skin of clouds, rests somewhere

on the roof of a carwash like a paper disk
I had cut with red-handled scissors as the solar eclipse
collected noon into a shadow
among the gray trees outside, beyond our desks.
Stravinsky (from his writings) dreamed of a young girl,

her erratic hands grabbing nothing,
wrapping the air in scarves around her neck.
I drive down the highway sparking with hubcaps
in the animal flight of plastic bags—here, ambulances
shriek every few minutes. I pull into a gas station,

wipe bird smears off my window with some paper.
Pump fumes smell like greasy hamburgers.
Your hair, your hair is red. The man is behind me,
his pale eyes smoothing my shoulders,
drawing a cold line under my T-shirt.

Your hair is red in the sun. No. Sky
bands the nearby Dollar Store window;
feeling followed, behind some junky trees I see a crane
lifting from the concrete, gold, the way a harp
unfolds in an orchestra—not a wing, but a thin wild sail.

Violinist

Once, there was a knife, a bone sliver
of wood, a crate packed with balls of white hair:
my mother's weaving loom,
unscrewed, growing out of cardboard boxes
like strange plants in the basement,
her voice returning to my shoulder.
Her words wrap around the shuttle,
darting it through the strings:

quiet knotted harp.

Now, backstage I rustle in my gown, worried, a dried flower
rubbing off leaves in a pantry, in darkness.

This is tuning: pinching
a black peg between thumb and index finger like a dead bee,
the moaning—
weak chairs creaking underneath guests,
then a perfect sound—my fingers slide between sofa cushions—
four silver quarters,   success,   Eratosthenes
painting sun triangles with poles stuck in sand.

The audience is an airplane shadow
spreading across chairs
like our house roof so close to O'Hare
that each engine scream
cast our bodies into statues for five seconds.

Now there is this moment:
when the slim canoe slaps against the dock,
empty, when the body must balance inside
petal-thin walls. An oar slides into the water,
grazes rock.
            I drift off, shoulders rowing:

a river bird, an ink-brush,
trees my father taught me to draw by standing under them.

This is why I spend years building stables
—finger-joints measured, solid,
strong enough to protect all of the horses.

Nestor

For we know what intelligence is hidden
                              —iii. 18

Throat rubbed raw from my violin, I pay in quarters
at the track and grip the painted railing
—win!—level with shivering horses
pounding the terra-cotta dirt: running, running, wet

stones around the bend, then animals
snorting and gasping, then forms

the churning surf allows almost dry
in the hair, in the water, in the flush of recall.

Lesson

Flames ice the grass. Nests of hornets
murmur in the smoke. Clay steams.
Horses snorting ash pass barebacked.
It is not enough to want to leave—
consider the tapestry knotted near the hearth,
the pots and pots of boiled lentils.

All of the nights breathing in that one place,
the dark room where dinner spices hang
above the face the way wind sucks in
through an open window. Lot fed the visiting angels
bread his wife flattened on a stone,
palm on stone, as the men of the city circled.

The men of the city want to fuck the angels.
Screaming horses pass Lot's wife as she climbs
the hill from the Valley of the Salt Sea—
the tents below lit up like blown glass.
All those nights breathing in that one dark room,
remembering: blood on the thighs, wet as tongued

saliva, blood staining the skin—
do not enter. Do not enter. On the hill,
Lot's wife heard her past self's
hair catching fire in the city.
This story is supposed to be a lesson,
someone could remind me. You should not

look for your past self: naked
below, below. Go back.
Get the woman out. The men want
to fuck the angels. A sheep's on fire now,
running. Turn back and get the woman
out of the room. Another horse passes.

Ash, the stairs must be ash now,
and empty. The snapping wood ribs of the room.
The cellophane lens heat casts.
The woman. There won't be any woman
in the wrong bed. She'll get out
so there won't be any woman on a hill.

There won't be any city burning behind,
hot on the back of her thighs. The sweat.
There won't— be any anyone— turn back, watch.

Watch for the Blind

Pearls, and what must seem incalculable
cuts, half-dozen arcing to the mid-six,
the remainders roughing a circumscription
to twelve—this ticking at the wrist
that swings among the clang of bottle-ringing.
The arcades are alive above the yellow-white water
sliding tethered boats closer to the pier.
I can see the woman, how she knows,
can even describe the boardwalk planks
somehow & the sand mauve in near darkness,

all the tents gapped in the new breeze,
slightly cold. The gears locked under glass
fillip a vein, the blood inside—this whole scene
kind of operatic with a fortune teller mumbling,
knuckles and scarves keeping something
from this passing into night. The woman
fumbles for the pearls put there with glue.
Silence is a guide at her elbow. A bicycle
clicks through an alley between bungalows.
But what can explain its disappearance?

Wandering Rocks

Some people say they like certain music without thinking.
In rehearsal one conductor yelled,
Don't ruin this temple, don't spit on this castle.
In Greencastle, Ireland, triangular stairs wear into the stones.
The tower is a chute darkening the dirt
where parents, angry about their daughter,

buried a man alive, his arms thinning to oak twigs.
We can pretend this is a moment in time,
if you like. The steering wheel had locked in the blue
Voyager van near the stench of Gary, Indiana,
and my mother coasted us to the shoulder,
a patch of Queen Anne's lace, weed flowers,

while my father pulled over the truck,
a rented U-Haul packed with family blankets,
her strong weavings, a sculpture with his own wisdom
tooth glued to it. But what I remember best
are two thick chains weighing down the German shepherds
that choked at us behind the auto garage.

Sun heated their necks metallic blue, and gravel chalk
collected on their muzzles. Is art more real
when it is described or named?
I watched a performance artist in college
pour gasoline on a piano someone dragged past the football field,
and she lit it with a match that sparked inside

the wood's holes where brass foot-pedals stick out.
Strings popped pitches—A, D#—and the grass
glowered, the crowd getting bored with how long it took
for the keys to explode yellow, collapse, the black back to lean,
and I stood near some composers, music students,
the last few watching. One said crassly *it's like Beethoven*—

chord-chord-chord-and chord and you think it is done, then—*chord*—
finished? No—*chord.* An event can be a parody the way nakedness
pretends to be naked as that morning
I touched the sun in my hair, pushed it
from my eyes, rubbed makeup off my eyelids,
felt my face, flushed and hot. The first door, out of his room,

led to stairs. The stairs led down. The morning was autumn,
when silver frost crusts the grass, the kind of morning
that I like to wake up to with my coffee,
sit by the smoky window, notice the cold tree
moving with things: one with rosy feathers crowning its head,
one I think looks like an egg dipped in dye,

one that is large and almost blue. I forget their names.
Is anything more real when it is described or named?
I confided in a friend and she told me, *he finished*
what he started, meaning, finished in you,
meaning that was what you wanted,

and then she was finished with me. That summer
I had rented a bicycle, rode one length
of an Aran Island, past huge intelligent cattle
blinking in the sun from behind low stone
fences and the walls of ruined houses where wind
wore the roofs away. The path followed the ocean
to one of the island's cliffs and a semicircle stone fort,

Dun Aonghasa, built so farmers could see invading ships.
I climbed through the short square opening in rock,
and the ledge was flat as the sky. The wall felt almost safe.
I lay my belly on the warm pink stone,
slid to the edge, put my hands where the rock
cuts down, curled my fingers over, thrust

my face out over nothing and water—
turquoise and yellow, crushing, glassy, up and up.
I smelled the spray, looked out where a finger
rubbed the horizon silver. Out there there were
no ships glittering—who would invade this small
farm island, with its stony fields, its pool of seals

on the other side of the land? The small round heads
looked like human swimmers, bobbing in water, disappearing,
reappearing, even smaller, even farther away.

Bluff

Forget about homing pigeons.
Send cadmium-feathered crested malimbes

to Conceptual Prison
down the street from 2218 Leavenworth—

where sapsuckers dash above wires,
frost-bite gray with dirt,

with hunger, these singleton pilots
performing nose-to-nose and nose-to-tail turns

beyond the cartilage skins of the windows,
the bricks and bricks and bricks.

I want to retire to an island,
alight all the candles lined up in their drawers

in the prison chapel, the alter cloth
shimmering the color of carp.

Johnny Cash asked the guards
if he could just have a glass of water

I heard in the recording from San Quentin prison.
And I am wondering where fire-fronted bishops nest,

stern plumes of feathers, a burning way of staring,
drawn in the sun of a book illustration?

Proteus

—his hands gleam with water or end up gripping the cannon bone of a frightened deer, or a long blue candle dripping hot wax down his arm.

It's like this, a spool of lace ribbon wound tight, taped to its own cloth, so you can work a little to unwrap it, place the loose end on the rug, run around the room, darting three times between the chairs until the quiet space is a white mess everyone wants to stick their fingers in.

There is also effect:

Rape of the Mind.

There were five red doors down the street across from the playground and the police station where the town cars line up like duck decoys. My door was the third one—when you knock a woman opens it and asks *who are you?* And then she leads you up the creaky stairs, because it is just an old house after all, and there is an office in a bedroom, maybe once a child's because there are still silver star stickers clumped on the ceiling, and you sit in a chair and the woman listens to you, then names it.

"I don't remember. I remember."

So in your car the steering wheel feels like bones. So when you lie flat on your bed you are a body. You think about death.

You remember being a fifteen-year-old body in a room filled with wasps. A woman calls your name and you play Brahms. You walk back to the dormitory through a park with a fountain.

The wet persistence of water on stone.
Stone moving in the light.

You could have left your violin in its black case, there in the park, but you brought it, and threw it on your bed.

So you sat in the orchestra, back where all of the violins' faces look like *little moons*. That is what one conductor announced. *Do not cross your legs under your chair.*

The ground is where you get your power, your balance.

You straightened your legs and raised the metal music stand, a blackened fan.

The Chorus Rubs on Children's Sunscreen

We grieve. We grieve. We crinkle the corners
of sheets in our fists, try to fold the cloth.
A battle flag. If there were candles,
flames would drip stalactites of blushed wax.
We know where the garbage bags are,
clean as unlicked envelopes, scented:
a knifed lemon. You there. We know
about you. You could be waking to an alarm.
Your pillow holds your dreaming brain.
You are allowed to be thoughtless, to live
in a normal way—wherever you are.
You walk to the market,
thinking in the freckled shade.
Flies bury stained-glass wings, blue,
in the moist locks of hair above your ears.
Or, you drive, strapping the triangle weave
of the seat belt across your heart.
Your heart can or cannot be heard
like a freight train pulsing the air outside
our childhood bedrooms.
The neighborhood kids assigned roles
in their games, and one child tried to spell
"hate" with a marker on a paper napkin:
I hat you.
        We protect our eyes.
Sunroofs cut the parked cars drooling oil
from their pipes.
          We protect our skin.
Smell. Bowls of grapefruit skins weigh the trash,
a system of scales:
            You.
You.
You are falling asleep somewhere.

Nausikaa

And we live far apart by ourselves in the wash of the great sea
At the utter end, nor do any other people mix with us
                                                        —vi. 204–205

Nothing happens here, but it might:
red bandannas group the men near the door,
and heat hangs around the metal baskets chiming
together as people bump past holding their week

in sheets. Nothing happens, but nests
of hair wind hatched shadows
around the legs of a linoleum table
where there is a stack of infant undershirts,

clean slices of bread on wine-blue pants.
A man stammers *no watch*,
holds his bare wrist to me. *Here.* Autumn
jackets smack and smack one porthole.

Two girls are chasing each other
around their mother's legs and tumble into
ribs of light folded within a blanket.
Through the window's fluorescence,

little white handprints appear. Cars could be swans
in an olive grove—but the streetlamps
look nothing like trees, these cars are not birds,
and the window rips with morning

like a sheet of aluminum foil.
We give ourselves to the current
of machines and wait together under three TVs:
in each, the same woman is making herself cry.

Cleaning Out the Lyre

Pour fifteen grains of rice into your hand
and guide the ice-white, jumping chips to the face
of your lyre, then to the cheekbone band,
a silhouette. Then in the f-hole lace—

yes, inside, the lining of willow-wood—*clean,*
clean rice. The dust's loose. The voice of rain
moves the trees that bow to the silver-green
lake where a horse and cart's loaded with chains

to secure the carp along the river road
and past the shop where Jean Baptiste's artists
plane the willow and sand the maple good
for ribs. Some unbraid white horsehair with mist

they spit, and a bone comb. Then they stretch,
unwrapping bread and cheese over a sketch.

After the Lotus

Sit in the narrow beak of the canoe and push the oar
against the green hands the current breathes against the frame.
Placid. Black pines opening at the water.

The wooden handles drag bugs scarring the water's silver
and now the sun steams the lake the way my mother and father exhale
an iron over their smooth blue shirts. My grandfather

showed me the doves in our yard,
the ones that look like opera singers filling their breasts
before exhaling, feathers gray not with dawn,

grieving in pairs, their tails swooping up
to the cracked ledge of our carriage house.
I imagine gold hay inside. In pairs, one knows

another: wrapping kitchen dishes in newspaper,
answering the telephone when it opens up
the night from its place on the piano.

Cyclops

All perspective is is a dot
you can plan on any page
and then draw solid cubes so a house

can hover above crayon spikes of grass.
I am afraid. I have seen sheep puff
like dandelions,

some spotting blue as though thumbs
pushed ink on their backs.
Farmers spray dye on the rams

so after rutting with ewes,
the used ones are marked.
The more a thing is investigated,

the more it burns. Light on paper.
A museum displays these photographs:
Paganini's ghost wearing a devil mask

pushing down on his violin,
and others, a serious girl,
hair parting her skull in half.

People show others how no one *is*
still there—turning a cold doorknob.
And how the more a thing is probed,

the more it burns. O it burns.

Aiolos and the Bag of Winds

And I endured it and waited, and hiding my face I lay down

—*x. 53*

When language fails, there is sound,
        wind chimes
and the rustling of potted ferns

growing near the screen door.
On this porch after school, I cared for a child
found in an empty factory,

her new father in the garden
among sugar snap peas rubbing together,
glimmering as though moving in rain.

Upstairs, the doll-sized nightgowns
were folded into squares
like canvas sails

pressed closed. I'd try to calm her.
She'd open her eyes, just aware of my voice,
the way my sister turns her head

to the car window, to Main Street's
orange words on signs,
the heavy trees spreading night around us.

She slides off her thumb ring, rubbing it,
balancing the silver circle
on one jean kneecap, the comb of her hand

behind an ear. My voice comes
from another place.
The parking lot is dim, ordered, and quiet.

Water Ballad

Assigned to a table with Kristin Johns
and gems tucked in a box.
Our washing spigot gleamed bronze,
dripping our Xerox:

Moh's Hardness Mineral Test.
A metal file and glass.
Her T-shirt stretched across her breasts.
We knew, the whole class.

"Do you want to see my baby?"
Kristin Johns asked.
"I got a picture of my baby
here in my bag."

Pearly talc is softer than gypsum,
but mirrors scratch both.
Gypsum looks like a rose blossom,
I dutifully wrote.

At thirteen I'd seen sonograms
from when Mom had Abbey.
At thirteen Kristin's sonogram
showed a ghostly baby.

Smoky quartz can crush talc,
a greasy white powder.
The baby's face was white as milk,
its fists closed on a ladder.

"My daddy says the baby's ugly,"
Kristin Johns laughed.
"He said my baby *is* ugly,"
Kristin Johns laughed.

She rustled open a Tastykake,
put the picture away.
The baby slept in its glossy lake
someplace far away.

Ballyhoo or Bulletin?

Cucumbers and goat cheese and basil,
this the gelding gave me in my dream,
set on a yellow plate in the mud while the horse
peered into the river, no roots or ragged rocks

erupting the surface like a rocket's nose
when wind edged the crispate veneer,
stilled. In my dream this creature loved me,
was me.
        There's a rule that I forget,

about twisted tube slides, though one kid
must be enserfed as lookout
the way a ballgirl or ballboy
will follow then pinch a wild fluorescent form

(popped from the can!) out of a metal fence.
Serve.
        I remember a bathroom mirror,
but not my face. I remember my photo,
but not the school, except for the idea of plants

alive in the cut bottoms of plastic bottles
we filled from a dirt bag and pushed in seeds of holy

moly!—black roots swelling invisible except for weight,
detectable shadow, when angled afternoon sun

met the dimness,
                and the white flowers . . .
maybe we waited too long for them, or didn't
get the message, Hermes: instead I grew broom-
rape, parasite herb, purple and scaled.

Circe's Notes

Socrates decided to be executed.
And the execution of art?

In a public garden, a tree
wears a skirt
          of hard green apples

with a white crescent bite
out of each skin.

I need more symbols
to hook into my ears.

Mirrors.
       At the hardware store
I bought big hooks.
               Swinging.

I like how the glass
captures swatches of my cheek.

Maybe I shouldn't have

taken the earrings off:

I wish I ripped his lips.

O my potbellied pig.

            I'll eat you.
And when I cook pig,

one pig cries and cries
           for another pig.

Oracle

A whale is in your future: hidden
under chopped-up water, and dumb.
The augurs know from the white-out
splashes, sea birds bobbing numbly
until lifting in a patch of wind.
They will land elsewhere altogether.
Gulls will cover the sand, skull-pale,
picking at nothing. All will turn black.
They will eat your trail of crumbs.
So this sounds invented?
So grackles will too descend:
oily blue plumage, each tail the wedge
of a sculptor's tool
you could pick up at a junk sale,
the driveway grouped
with people slow-moving
past milk crates of wild—
the sinews no longer hold the flesh
and bones together—
linseed-greased and more
and more naked, dolls.

Ossuary

But inside the bone museum, go in, go in, show the girl
    behind the glass desk
your ticket stub. This ossuary smells like the inside of a violin,

an expectancy of sound when the tawny summer shoes of that family
    pad the stones.
A monk boiled people he couldn't bury during the Plague,
    then the Crusades,

and these are the bones—he pulled the chalk ends apart and refitted
    the knobs of arms
to make this museum, thirty-thousand bodies used like matchsticks.

Skulls huddle along the ceiling, or between the ceiling beams
    and roof above
the bone chandelier made from all that's left. Squint, the place
    could be limestone

or ocean-worn coral, pocked, smooth, grown together. The roof
    umbrellas us.
Our cameras spark here and there—dull brown beetles lighting up
    beyond us.

Remember home, how the insects sparkle the peonies,
the chiffon, bulbous-headed flowers bowing to the alley of the church—

when building the choir room, construction workers split shovels
    into graves,
the tombstones dating to when the town faced the river,
    when trading boats

docked, unloaded, and some of the brick homes honored with metal
    date badges
face the water still, having survived the floods that lifted soil
    from the banks,

that silenced the town, rose to the tips of wrought-iron fences
    and covered the burials,
the stone markers later cemented with the bricks in the decorative
    courtyard

behind the building where people stop now to shake rain from umbrellas,
silver blades opening like jellyfish blooming in the electric water.

The Sirens

Pilot whales beach their black bodies
on sandbars off the Cape. With my grandparents,

I watched the dying on TV in August,
when tourist children poured more sun

onto the whale fins with neon play-buckets
of warm water, tried to push them out,

push them out past the stripes of gleaming
snails but the whales kept coming in again at high tide,

and when water bled away from their heavy forms
they cried soft dog noises that humans also

make from a place in the ribs that opens
a chamber, a cathedral, where an echo

echoes and loses itself. Ear training involves singing,
knowing how to sing a series of pitches in your mind

before your mouth finds strange leaps
in sound with the tongue and throat, not a melody,

these facts to learn. Stuff your ears with wax,
fall asleep on the deck of a motorboat

near the jagged granite rocks people arrange
into jetties to guide the land. *Guidance, what*, people say,

some women need and *they had it coming*. I remember
braiding the hair of a friend's doll by myself in her bedroom,

and the sheer curtains whipped rain against the walls
and then the tornado sirens howled, first one,

then another, suburban wolves, as all the nearby
towns called and called to one another.

The babysitter downstairs told me I heard
nothing and flipped the radio on, piled flashlights

near her sandals, so my friend and I checked
the basement but yellow clumps of sewage

had backed up to the bottom step, strewn flowers
of toilet paper to clog the wheels of the pool table,

so upstairs we made sure the cathedral windows
opened to trees, close to the house, so dark,

and we sat listening, knowing from school that when
the storm comes, you have to let the wind in.

Scylla and Charybdis

1.

It is this way with remembering: a door
is a sketch on butcher paper,
and the artist's black frame bed
actually within the bone-white
Egon Schiele museum belongs there
the way horses eating
pull together along Pennsylvania
highways like a pile of my friend's shoes.
Where I once lived, birches twirled
green fans. Here I am
again: our back gate was left unlatched
and the school bus's white eyes opened
for my brother and me on our patch of road,
the rust streak where a man scooped up our dog.
Walls seem to fall into each other and catch our hair.

2.

The hot beach towel is soft in the sand.
My wet knees stick to the slippery magazine
pages of fern dresses, the slivered jaws of women
who lean absently on wrought iron lace.
My sister and I peel the leg openings of our bathing suits
away from skin, measuring honey.
Our grandmother's thumb-speck
fishing hat moves as she checks the wind and holds a toy
red spool, grabs the kite's bone shoulders, fights it,
lets go—I am reminded of the way dancers spin
sweat in the blued light, their mouths
taking in air as though they are singing.
There in the wings behind a netting
of pulleys: a flat tree trunk, the prow of a ship,
waiting for the machine of memory.

Oxen of the Sun

They cut away the meat from the thighs
$$\text{—}xii. \ 360$$

In a story, the farmer leaves his flock,
tromps through the tall grass, nearly braiding it
with his black boots. He hears something
and walks until he finds it, folds the muddy hooves
against his belt, and takes the thing to the shelter:
there is water, knives, a flat cold stone
rubbed with blood. In another story, a man's hands
move over the air between his legs. I notice the raw
slabs of meat marbling his mouth. And still his hunger.
He's not listening to what I'm saying, the bottle empty.
He's smiling. Someone says, *Flip, flip. The blood is rising.*

Standing Still

A bent arm from the cardboard whiskey box
packed with plastic dolls almost hooked one man's
pant cuff and the peach mattress staggered to the porch
of the house that breathed out all our things,
tired in the hot sun. A soft couch
collapsing with flat cushions baked in the grass.
Everything looks cheap outside each time
we pack it, carry it to the back of a truck,
drag it upstairs in another house—
door propped open, boxes wrecked like bottles
along the new driveway where mermaids would have lived
before I stopped drawing. The last time
I remember their blue faces appearing
lonely in tar, black-ribboned clouds
pulled breathing trees close to the house.
In Northern Ireland I stood in the ruins
of Dunluce Castle and learned about a mermaid
cave hollowing limestone under the teal water.
One night when rain rinsed the castle's stones,
its kitchens cracked away from the cliff,
showering the night water with dust,
iron kettles of porridge, and all of the cooks.
A cobbler stayed standing in the far corner of the vanished
room, maybe licking a spoon or gripping a sash
rippling empty over the cold sea-spray.
The Countess of Antrim refused to sleep in the castle,
so she moved out that night, taking what she needed:
terrestrial globes that once peered from her observation towers
so she could touch the ground with one finger,
guide its spin, then clamp the moving earth tight in her hands.

Kalypso

. . . days to be endless . . .
                        —v. 136

Into the mountain navel
we rode down the shaft
through the tunneled air
as the anthracite miner breathed

cracking gasps behind the helmet
light fading ahead into a forever
island the way my flashlight would beam
at blue whips of birches toward some stars. No-

thing. And what exists continues blandly
with a longing
to collect the pink clouds
smearing a liquor store window—
my ID in another's hands,

the silk almond opening
of my wallet, and *inside*, blood.

The Chorus at the Pit

Our last bruised apple rolls among the hard onions. Our memory
is a refrigerator box upside-down in the grass: our castle.
Even last week, when our uncle said his friend owns Thomas Edison's voice,
we could imagine it, stored between a silver spoon collection and a row
    of shot glasses
stamped with *London* or empty beach chairs. So we have our canvas
bags stuffed with plaster masks and decaying horseshoe crabs—
each hollow rib cage crusted in sand grains—and the last white houses
standing, vacant, in Centralia, Pennsylvania, wreathed in smoke
like early morning fog settling on fence tips, where to get rid of garbage
someone threw a match in a trash pit, igniting an anthracite vein.
Fire races through underground mines. Roads buckle above ground,
fold into earth so poisoned that most people flee. Even the government
    has given up,
ignoring coal crevices, caves, the flames spreading wild for miles.
Enormous heart. The trees are ruined. We see barren soil
exhale shawls of gauze. We breathe the vapor. Our signs read *Collapse*.

Spoken from the Maze Daedalus Made

It is all a misunderstanding. The car tucks its envelope shadow between other metal domes, reflecting the dim orange lights that wash the floor in a gloss. Around, around the levels, C5, the growling ventilation fans remind me to walk with intent in the garage. Know where to go: this is an important lesson—each time I learn it. In the coffee house swept by red curtains where I often get the chipped *Queen of Hearts* coffee mug, a man tells me he is bidding on Jerry Garcia's toilet—small and porcelain white, no shit stains, just something to screw on his walls under its authentication certificate. Like Duchamp, steal ready-mades from people with wine-stained teeth: in Columbia, street vendors sell iguana eggs boiled in salt, punctured with string, hanging the way only eggs can hang—smelling of rot. Eat reptile flesh. Eat any object left in a warm crumpled ball of aluminum foil on the train seat. Red red sauce. Before I was born, my parents rented the downstairs apartment to a man who never threw out his nail clippings, the yellow shells stuffed in sandwich bags, tucked inside empty corn cans, lying under months of cigarette ash dusting the *Chicago Tribune* stacked daily to the ceiling in teetering gray walls, enough words for anyone, even for me to cut up and steal until my hands cramp open. But continue, continue about how I pressed my first carnation under *The Complete Works of William Shakespeare*, heavy enough, and the boy drew pencil mazes on notebook paper for me to trace, and now he is so fucked up his eyes cannot focus beyond his matted bangs. I jab a wall with my elbow. The lesson, learn where to go, open the similar doors of all the rooms I've lived in and end up in my own closet, cushioned by stacks of towels smelling of sweet chemicals. Then eavesdrop on my neighbors. Can I hear them breathing through the wall? Eavesdrop on myself, listen to my damp feet sticking to tile, pushing footprints, wet, that evaporate, of course, of course they do. So breathe on the mirror—a tuft of cotton brushes over the mouth. Do not admit *I am lost*. Stack glasses so they smash in the kitchen, so there are heavy footsteps cracking the stairs, so a broom misunderstands the floor: *brush, brush, brush.*

Rations

After sleeping all day
on a friend's pullout,
we buy canned food.

All the bagged pastries
sweating in the convenience

store window face the scaffolding
of the 7 she takes to the schizophrenics,

the woman no one believes.

Cats sulk under the dust ruffle
in the apartment where we wash
a handful of plastic forks.

The temple—I keep remembering
the woman tearing white bread
for a cluster of mottled pigeons.

How she disappeared
through a red door.
How she returned with a broom.

Disguised, Athena Says . . .

Hey, I wish these jeans would zip.
That woman cups her daughter's
rosy pear shoulder and pulls the girl

under a tacked-up sheet, the cornflowers
on the curtain dividing our stalls of stiff carpet.
I love this thrift store. The girl is gone

again—there she goes, tumbling, her head
wrapped in a T-shirt wrinkling pink sparkled letters.
I am tired of following my owl along the river

in these boots—and look what parking lots did
to the heels, from walking and walking,
so my bed even smells like the heap of dirt

I scooped from a hole by the porch
for that new birch, or was it a blue pine?
The girl's foot kicks the curtain and she hangs

a banana-sized slipper from her toes.
The thing is soulless, looks infectious.
Where have those slippers been?

The gardener also asked this in the *Red Fairy Book*
while the sisters slept all day in their row of beds
having lined up their slippers, the toes damp

from sneaking out and running through silver forests.
The leaves were hammered scraps of metal.
The gardener saw, concealed by a cloak in a raft:

the violins, finger cymbals, light and hips and incense
ghosting the muslin castle curtains where the women danced.
In the tired morning, he dug a hole under their window,

filling the dirt with a fern or a sweet-pea.
He knew what he was doing, hiding in his clothes.
One morning my brother's friend

wore my sneaker—he shoved his huge foot
into the black leather, his other foot in his own shoe,
tripping and awkward on the sidewalk past the corner

where the three temples are. I saw him.
When he returned to Olympos,
dumping his books by the door, he kicked both

shoes off—mine was the one gold with dust.
It was mine: the woods, the falls.
As someone would write about me,

she bound upon her feet the fair sandals,
gold and immortal, that carried her over the water.

Performance

This bird is just imitating people imitating crows
　　　　　　　　　　　　　　　　　　—*Why Birds Sing*

The story involves a whole village kept busy
making earthenware jars while the hurricane
a hundred miles offshore kicks up the oily green ocean
and the only two people who won't escape
are sweating in an abandoned stable the rain slashes.
They are naked and touch the dirt floor with their fingers,
thinking someone is about to pull open the door.
Characters can't know the real crisis: Dorothy doesn't remember
Lion being the farmhand who pulled her from the pigpen
before she glittered the dead witch's shoes—
glint, glint, glint—back to where she began.
But in real life, the cherry picker parked across from the post office
extends its silver basket. The tiny human figure
looks like he stands in a toothbrush cap up there
and he's reaching for the black seam dangling the stoplights
when a car hits the truck and the crane swerves the man,
and he falls. He dies. What then? We can only control
some stories: babysitting, I would turn three pages at once
during the fifth bedtime book until the girl sitting on my lap
asked about the train and why this time the conductor didn't wait.
I would be caught, like now, when I am nowhere but pretending to be
standing in the Pittsburgh Aviary watching flamingos
step through a pond, the white plastic pipes churning, bubbling the surface.
One cartoon pink leg lifts a wet claw, dips it back,
stepping into the ventilated wind with the others
like plastic flamingo lawn ornaments our friend staked in his lawn
and switched around at dusk—sometimes three turning their backs to one,
sometimes all seven forms seeming to proceed to the curb in the fog—
as though the neighbors would have to consider
the ornaments becoming birds and moving themselves.

This is suggested plot, though, like when a child
asks you to keep the bedroom door open
after you tuck her in so (you think) the vertical strip of light
can illuminate the bookcase next to her pillow
when she really wants the lion tucking his paws under his mane
and guarding the foot of her bed to know
he can exit by pushing his nose on the door.
Now I am listening to a white-crested laughing thrush
chortling up by the aviary's skylights
and a blue parrot muttering at the blank clouds:
"I shot a man in Reno just to watch him die,"
which could be a climax if there was a story
followed by a rainy walk to the car,
the powder-gray bats I've never seen here before
dipping from oak to oak as randomly as meteors.

Finding Eumaios at the Return

Inside the enclosure he made twelve pig pens
next to each other, for his sows to sleep in

—xiv. 13-14

The swineherd feeds them: carrot scraps, a pat
of butter, leather gloves, corn from a dented can,
brittle bones of a dill stalk clumped in an owl pellet
chunk of bread, translucent apricots, each a mouth
"o" of pleasure, the hunger of the body.
Kids throw tennis balls and the jokes on Popsicle sticks
into the park's creek. Description. If there is no need to know
about a place, then here: in rain, leaves
the color of sand pressed the street curb,
slicked sidewalks in the dark. Then, some mornings
the air smelled sugary with varnish before the factory
stopped shipping out beds and closed, the wood
planks blackening where the slow trucks would load,

unload. Dogs still squat there by the fence, loyal to sticky
grass, even in rain. Even in sweat, and in a piss
brown stall. I am too tired now to think
through myself in a mirror, the gas station
window, the dip of a spoon. Gold
dirt ashed air as I watched horses being
prepared for jousting at an autumn festival.
One horse pawed a hoof in the dust, poured rippling
hair to the earth. A man fed it from a pail,
rubbed the body calm. Now a water tower
beams heavy white from the corn as stars
shift over this field and the next one, washed
familiar with the egg-manure smell of sows.

Penelope's Firebird Weft

Red linen wings: orange, long, draping the back of shoulders like a rain-coat. It is not the dust, not human ashes in vessels heavy with gray teeth and a chip of bone. Bring out the pencils and remake a self. For the school play, we repainted the stage black every year. When the Doctor missed his entrance because he was backstage pressed between the full-length mirror and the curtain rod hanging with zip-up calico dresses, his mouth open and warm, someone had to keep talking, saying *drawing room, drawing room,* become the strange person who suddenly had an opinion about scalloped potatoes, three-volume novels, Stravinsky, who wrote *forte, forte, forte, forte* five times in the end of *L'oiseau de feu,* louder than any voice, loud enough for the trumpets to crack their pealing calls, look—look at the wings, look the ashes part, look, the sharp eyes, the feathers open, shake the tree leaves like me, the way I was, walking to school in the light carrying the folded backpack loose across my shoulders. A chip of bone. I am waiting for the cue, the thin baton you can buy from a catalog and practice with. Grinding my teeth down, practicing scales so my fourth finger can become strong. When I buy a yellow rose, when I answer the telephone, when I stand on a drainpipe, when I think the blues in the stained glass window glow true, when I open my mouth, I see white smoke, smoke next to the diesel truck, smoke inside my red sweater folded in a drawer, smoke rising from my dirty underwear heaped in the corner, smoke trapped in my unmade bed, empty and warm, a nest of linen.

Foyer

Twice in your life you will breathe Caesar's last breath
sucked in whirring gold and glass revolving doors,
the draft grazing these stone lions closing lips over teeth.
Go up the steps and you know why you're here:
murals of John Singer Sargent's flushed, draped, back-lit women
turning faces toward the pan flute, to each other's closed mouths,
to the lemons growing green to white in the brushed leaves.
This is a library. A sheet hangs down one wall.
Taped-up signs read: *In Repair, In Repair, In Repair.*
You are noticing carved gremlins or cupids, whatever they are,
trapped at the ceiling, fat legs bicycling the air.

Chorus: A Museum Is Under Construction

Coronations and jousting tournaments.
A hundred years to build—in medieval Europe
there was *no precedent*
for secular interiors on such
a large scale, and the peaked whale ribs

of the roof swallow us.
The vaulting, more sculpture than roof,
is like interlocked and twisted hands.
We've been there, but now we're reading books.
We sit as though on a lover's jacket.

Our lover could be drawing the Smithsonian
museums on the National Mall.
Bicyclists and Italian greyhounds
pass us with paintbrush shadows.
Our lover's hair would shade the page.

This cathedral's castle glass up there—
slashed milky slits and gold-dashed
hands of the clock, rosettes where the three
and six would be—is not the Tudor Palace,
begun in 1514, or the gilded mirror

we saw tilting the room above the writing
desk and opal-inlay bird-footed chair
pushed underneath. People were shorter then,
their beds were also shorter—see the canopy
bed between the second droop of the velvet

ropes, the museum's conscious effort
at consciousness, keeping us away
from flowering sedge, and the false
colors of the photographed stars,
and lunar craters sloping—a black lake—

as though hands had pushed and pushed the moon?
Let's pretend we understand things.
Now the empty lakes are systems of rays.
Now let's read maps of Jupiter's satellites
or *A Beginner's Guide to Hieroglyphs*,

drawing them, not what they mean:
the vulture's angle at the back of the head
can be explained by how the features
in that region behave, vaulting
as water fans out, disturbed.

Violin Shop

Instruments hang from the ceiling,
stiff necks, bodies burnished gold,
curved like pheasants, mute swans, a rare condor,
so valuable that symphony musicians
borrow these forms only for specific concerts,
such as *Scheherazade*, where a violin solo
draws the hushed audience
inside itself like rows of oars
sliding on the flat deck of a Phoenician ship.
In the shop, luthiers worry—they wipe
varnish on their apron pockets.
Glass pots gleam yellow with boiled glue,
and slips of tan horsehair fan the worktables;
the silver tools small enough to fit inside my mouth
cannot make *Guarneri del Gesu* speak.
Rumors say the three-hundred-year-old
violin hid beneath the bed of a man in Spain
while a bullet spat his wet blood:
a clean red arc across the floor. Black *f* slits
angle in an "antagonistic" way—the violin mutters,
complains under the chin of Berlin
Philharmonic musicians. I read this
in the *Chicago Tribune*. The shop owners
stood over the wood instrument, praying
for its voice, they brewed coffee,
rubbed its body with swatches of velvet,
then they called a man, an exorcist,
who probably laid the violin
down on the stock market page
as if it was a pumpkin, round,
hairy inside with seed-pulp, and chanted,
hollowing out its cavity: the voice that laughed at Bach,
groaned through Tchaikovsky's concerto

that usually runs so fast trees blur,
that spoke out loud longer than you
or I ever will and wanted to comment
finally on how things really are, was cured.

The Myth of Philomela

This autumn, Tereus catches sex.
Philomela fills her backpack with books and apples.
Even in rain, she walks to class
without a jacket, under trees yellowing
gray in the October blur.
Masks appear in the college town's stores.
Tereus likes the idea of Philomela
carrying waist-high pencil drawings
of her hand while she struggles
with an umbrella,
flattening the paper against a thigh.
Looking at her, he can see himself
already inside of her, but waits

for her to wipe her violin
to set the trap—knocking on her bedroom door
soberly to ask if she will be with him. Then.
No. He sits on her bed, notices
ink brushes soaking in a cup.
Entering would mean possessing this energy,
her shoulder blades slipping through the straps
of her concert dress, he imagines.
So he stages a kidnapping, so to speak,
makes sure she's out, his friends helping
by bothering her, and she shouts
something at Tereus, who says, *Come,*
touching the feathery wisps

uncaught by her ponytail,
let's take a walk, and she can see the moon
above the other bar across the street.
Philomela believes another version of herself
will visit this discussion, as an older sister.
Tereus would be committed to the whole
of this sister self, and they would
visit her father together.
Philomela can barely stand.
And she's inside his apartment—
he has her. Memory obscures it.
Except for a week the
pain in walking, and in sitting

during class on the edge of a chair.
Her sorrow feels as though she'd swallowed nettle.
She challenges—would challenge—him with truth.
The rumors begin circling
as though she'd died. He's taken her tongue.
Its stump throbs in her mouth
while the tongue itself murmurs somewhere.
In her room, she stays awake
unwinding shadows from an image,
preparing its threads for a textile: half-sketch, half-song,
the desk lamp lighting the window.
The myth of Philomela
is that the message wove with ease.

Ithaca

—*adapted from Joyce's* Ulysses, *17: 2013–2018*

"*Ever you will wander,*

selfcompelled,

to the extreme limit of cometary orbit,

beyond the fixed stars and variable suns and telescopic planets,

astronomical waifs and strays,

to the extreme boundary of space,

passing from land to land,

among peoples,

amid events.

Somewhere imperceptibly hearing and somehow reluctantly,

suncompelled,

obey the summons of recall . . ."

In the Chapter "Rodin in Love"

Rodin asks her to mold the feet and hands.
Sitting cross-legged on the rough wood panels,
rubbing the gummy clay warm, modeling a palm,
a thumb, the whiskered crease at the base of the nail.
Does it matter which embracing, naked forms
grasp each other's lust with her hands, not his?
She gave up her own form
experiments to shape the heels of his bodies.

After an Art Institute visit for school,
we all took a boat tour of Lake Michigan's dam,
wore safety vests like sandwich boards
and looked at the yellow bellies of the dead
fish slipping through the motor's wake.

I can smell the fresh salmon
steaks, salty through plastic wrap,
and the peach curls of frozen shrimp packed in Styrofoam
disks on the market's shelves.
The wet-pink contained sweat-salt,
the leg-crusts caught in each other,
the blunt brainy heads pressed to heads—all so strong
I almost pick up each cold, labeled, priced
sea-meat and take it home, remembering standing
in the sandy parking lot where shellfish farmers
or somebody had dumped pounds of clamshells
stinking and jeweled with fat jade flies:
I slid some of the chalky shards in my sack,
zipping in their moist, wet-can smell, their me-smell.

Rose

Oh Rose, Thou Art Sick
                    —William Blake

What is it about truth, images of truth?
The American committee for the 1889 Paris Exhibition

rejected *The Last of the Buffalo,*
Albert Bierstadt's panorama:
                              romantic West, pink-skied,
the clouds brushed as though sitting on glass,
the humble brown animals
                              eating and standing, too romantic.
What is it about truth, images of truth, like the body:
                              Mapplethorpe's banned photographs,
metallic and sculptural and sweating, these forms perfect as sand dunes
    in rain.

                    ~

The man sitting behind me drags his coat sleeve across a newspaper.
I think he is from somewhere in West Africa—his voice lifts like voices

on the bus
              bringing the night shift to the hospital,
the workers gossiping in cotton pastels

while the strip mall flashes illuminations—their cheekbones,
bodies washed in green.

His voice: *Always going to be my own way in this life.*
And: *Are you listening to me?*

                    ~

There is nakedness here,
not in the coats draped over our chairs,
but in being here.

A woman shuffles her mismatched shoes
past my window again
waving her cigarette distractedly,
a bubble wand fizzing
soapy ash. Being naked
has to do with being
watched:
          my friend told me about the man
in her hospital because his heroin needle
broke off inside one of his arm's purple holes—

puffy swollen skin. He tried to claw the metal out.

The room,
          jars of black ear speculums
                                  sunk in sterile liquid,
fistfuls of paper-wrapped tongue depressors,
                                  was her space.

I'm clean. He squinted at her. *Hey, look at you*
sticking out your hip,

cunt.

She splayed one hand over her clipped-on name.

        ~

In the Dark Ages, monasteries kept roses alive for medicinal purposes.
A man stands on the corner now among white plastic buckets,
the kind sand or mop wash holds down,

blowing dozens of rippling cellophane-wrapped magenta-flamed
roses,
tight buds opening at the tops
to velvety mashes of petals
you can muffle your lips into
and breathe
or not breathe.
He waves the swaying dots of color at cars.

I've read about dynasty rose gardens that in Chinese history
slicked parks with pale petals—
                              so many roses
the roots needed to be plowed under for fields of rice.

This afternoon no one wants these buckets of roses: rot-soft
urn-shaped insides
                    soaked in dye to delay blackening.

                    ~

Oh Rose, thou art sick,
                    William Blake illuminated in blood

ink so the words age on the print,

and death or sexual desire
or both
find *crimson joy* in *dark secret love*
and kill it, kill it, kill it.

The man, still behind me, says, *money*
and *no, no, no, no, no.*
His newspaper crackles closed.
I am beginning to think

I should walk to the self-storage warehouse
I pass every morning: glass walls

allowing me to see three floors of cobalt blue
nearly garage doors, padlocked,

obviously like options or even pasts.

I remember the story where the prince must choose which door to open:
the princess, or the tiger.

Which?

Behind which door, death? And behind which door, the chance of death?

~

The sign fluoresces *Private Self Storage* and on the first floor
potted spider plants dangle wanly in the darkening window.

The desk's pressure-treated surface blares and the room lacks chairs.
In my imagination the room means the desk versus you.

And which private selves are you going to leave with us today?

In my imagination I don't ask how big each room is
or how long a lease runs for each version of the body.

Plato had written about selves,
how the actor truly becomes the mask.
I relish the masks of the Sande Women Secret Society
of the Pende People in Liberia and Sierra Leone:

wood folds of neck-flesh
filled with power and filled with wealth,
the burnished round cheeks,
having sucked in the wind, holds it there, and when a man
rapes a girl or tries to choke his wife,

the women in these masks

screaming behind the carved expressions

collect branches and reed whips
and switch his back, punish the man,
make him sorry he lived.

~

I will keep the self who relishes these masks
but not the self who looked away when the Puck-like
middle-school girl/boy,
hair falling over his or her nose, crouched left
of the automatic doors at the drugstore—she or he

set the sensor off
so the doors whished open & shut,
open & shut
    as though individual shoppers trafficked through
and he or she grinned crazily,
high on something—

yes, I would choose to store away the self who stopped thinking then.

~

What is it about rejecting truth, images of truth?

Night was in my dream and a concrete dam
collected the ocean—
     I could hear the water swishing,
rushing, before I saw the wetness.

Then searchlights shone yellow across dirty patches of waves churning
green froth and whale-black glitter.

Silence was night,
was nothing.

And I chose the cracked tar parking lot:
empty paintings of parallel bars.

We begin to die
the moment we choke on our first gasp of air.

~

Or, instead of going to the beach at night
I took a cold shower,
                              waiting in the hostel's hallway
holding a towel and my shirt
while the cold Atlantic sky
slowly spun its crown of stars
above the moving, washing, near water.
Sweeping pink and green rays shot through the stars: Angel
Fire. Angel.

            Accepting your own body is knowing
anyone at any time can stand behind you,
wrap hands below your jaw,
the weight at your throat,

like my high school teacher
who did that to us for practice:
                              What will you do? What will you do?

Whip around, break his hold against both your forearms?

Or, freeze, accept your naked body,
and separate some ancient self from this?

~

Body that you remember when you wake,

pull a shirt over your head,
layer your legs in socks and jeans.

And face your self that you scent and rub with a wet towel.

When my mother was younger than I am,

she took the train from New Jersey to Penn Station,
her zip-up leather portfolio almost the length of her legs.

She clutched it against her ripped coat.
A man tried to pull it away—
                                        pencil self-portraits inside
protected between translucent sheaths of tracing paper.

Who would want these?

And there's the man conversing with himself
at the table
              slanted with sun behind me.
It must be hard to find such a good listener —

nodding, sighing, sometimes disagreeing
worriedly with the empty chair.

Tinsel Halo

Sun wraps the other balconies in wet wax paper—these apartment towers,
trees flickering wetness, holding air, moving air through nests of leaves.

Pencils could have sketched that radio tower fading in clouds soaking
    the almost
light when the sun catches up with my mood, too late for the comical
    mail truck,

jewelry box on wheels, hurrying past the back fins of the cars'
    exhaust pipes,
like opera binoculars peering at the dumpster. The soul has just enough time

to take a bookmark out of M. C. Escher's Etchings—photographic insides
    of castles
where insistent people march up flights of steps warping up the wall, a fisheye

lens curving the earth—or Picasso, the part about his desperate Blue Period
in Paris, where he'd lead his models upstairs and they'd step from dresses,

lie down, knees opening, hair undone and tangled in blue clouds
around their kohl-rimmed, wide, bored eyes, and they'd exhale cigarette
    figures

of smoke, the sun moving the indigo window's shadows across their feet
    and then
they'd sleep: crushed pigment and water. Like carnation stalks soaking
    blood dye

up to petals and the fringe explodes! The sky. At the ocean. The tidewater
    as warm as the twist
from the tap you wash your hands with, and a fishing vessel slits its razor
    shiver of a wake,

that lip of white against the green glass veins pulsing the water, pushing, pushing the body that lies on its back and stays here and stays here, stays here.

Cosmos

A peacock is rumored to pace
the rose bushes in Vojan Park
and I'm reading silk tags
that measure shoulder bone
to beneath the breast.
Sequins pooling my hands
are pond green, decadent as dance
costumes we ordered from catalogues.
We wore olive canvas suits,
fluttery skirts, and gold glitter
stripes to exaggerate brass
buttons: *heel, toe, heel, toe,*
march, march, march.
And we saluted the flag,
wherever it happened to be,
twirling, whipping our noses
to the corner of the studio—
our foreheads seeming still.
But this, this dressing stall
curtain lets in too much light.
Women brush its woven panels,
waiting—the clacking of hangers,
translucent, some hanging glassy
almost-torsos. Some entirely human
forms can be universally understood,
like outlines chalking an alley
while the real body, swaddled in sheets,
is lifted and carried away.
And outside of this is Prague,
Prague's horses, poppy-red
masks tracing their sinuses,
and the stairs that drop underground
every shuffling hour to bars,

and that man rushing from a grocer's
tucking bread under an arm.
When I look in the mirror again,
I push my breasts with my palms,
take them away, and then my friend
in the next stall slides her curtain.
Another pair of feet and it closes.
How will this shimmer
feel underneath all my shirts?
Will I catch the hook behind
and wear it for a while and shove it
in the trash, in Vojan Park,
in the gardens of the Monastery
of the Discalced Carmelites?
Taken by the Order of Virgins?
A statue of a man striding on a fish's back
greets you there under a weeping willow.
The man was not a hero.
But his tongue still pumped blood
when his body was unearthed—
truth in the way of a mystic,
an explosion of cosmos,
petal zings lisping above pale stalks.
But those flowers do not grow
in Vojan Park. One spring
we planted a packet of these seeds.
The torch color leapt up our fence,
a threshold of spots
dividing the quarry road
and home. Cosmos. My body
already the pigment.
My mouth opening.
O those cars—

suncompelled,
obey the summons of recall...

Other Books in the Crab Orchard Series in Poetry